IN PURSUIT OF THE HEADLESS CHICKEN

IN PURSUIT OF THE HEADLESS CHICKEN

Networking for Business in Any Economy

Trent Humphries

Strategic Introductions
2221 Justin Road 119-342
Flower Mound, TX 75028
www.StrategicIntroductions.com

Illustrations by Trent Humphries
Book design by GoodMedia Press

The text in this book is set in Futura and Cambria.

Manufactured in USA

ISBN: 978-0-9976255-0-9

To Uncle Art who gave me the job, my dad who asked Uncle Art to hire me, to the headless chickens that taught me so much and to my wonderful wife, who, after all these years of marriage still loves me even if I am still chasing headless chickens

CONTENTS

INTRODUCTION   9

KNOW YOUR COMPETITION   15

NEVER PLAY OUT OF POSITION   23

TILTING THE FIELD OF PLAY   31

BE FLEXIBLE, AND HAVE TWO MAPS   49

TRUST & MAKING DEPOSITS   59

MENTORING AND RELATIONSHIP CAPITAL   73

SPEED IS OF THE ESSENCE   85

RANDOMNESS AND SERENDIPITY   97

KNOW WHEN TO FOLD 'EM   105

CONCLUSION   113

ABOUT THE AUTHOR   117

APPENDIX ONE   121

APPENDIX TWO   127

INTRODUCTION
Separation Anxiety

IF THERE IS ANYONE ON THIS PLANET WHO UNDERSTANDS the well-worn phrase, "Running around like a chicken with his head cut off," I am that person.

At the tender age of nine, I began my education in the fine art of chasing down busy executives and decision-makers for meetings that would benefit everyone involved. Sometimes nature is our best teacher, and the lessons learned at Clary Poultry & Egg in Lubbock, Texas equipped me to effectively pursue clients, make valuable connections and create business deals.

The career I enjoy today of building relationships that connect clients to decision-makers in corporations and organizations for critical first meetings was born on the loading dock of that poultry plant. To fully understand the principles that will meet your needs, I must take you back to Clary Poultry & Egg, nature's classroom, where these principles were first learned.

A poultry plant is all about processing chickens, from live ones in the crates to packaged ones at the supermarket and every gross step in between. My station was at the initial stage of that unsavory process where the chickens were pulled out of the crates and their necks were wrung, resulting, sometimes, in a quick and certain death. I know, I know, that's horrible, but it happened. Maybe today they do something more humane, but I doubt it.

Uncle Art, owner and sole decision-maker of Clary Poultry & Egg, paid me 50 cents an hour. I received another 50 cents for every headless chicken I caught before it reached the highway, which equates to about $3.80 per chicken in today's dollars.

People who create jobs are the lifeblood of any economy. The guy who created my job was Bud. He was responsible for ensuring a live chicken never made it onto the conveyor belt and past the canvas flap into the processing area.

Occasionally Bud would get overly zealous about his calling. He'd put a little too much effort into the wringing of the chicken's neck, and the result would be a headless scrambling bird. Or perhaps Bud would be distracted, and a chicken with its head still intact, but scared senseless, would be dropped. Either way, the game was afoot when the chicken was loose. This is why it "sometimes" resulted in quick and certain death. The genesis of this story is in the "sometimes."

Here is how the process played out from the point of separation. When enthusiasm or distraction would get the best of Bud, a headless and, therefore, sightless bird would literally hit the ground running. My job was to catch the feathered rocket before it made it to the highway. This was a total distance of about 75 feet across a parking lot that usually held three or four of the workers' cars.

Those headless chickens still had a lot of life left in them and, given the chance, would run and run. The problem was that State Highway 82 passed close by and was just a short distance for the feathered sprinters. The highway was generally busy during the working hours of the poultry plant,

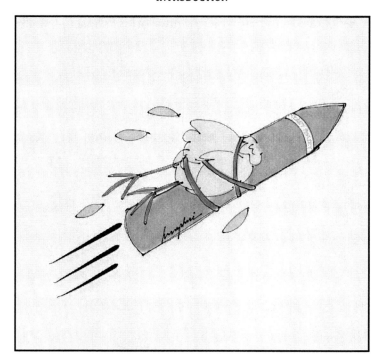

and the opportunity for a chicken to become road kill was high. A high-speed and extremely confused headless chicken darting onto the highway was, for some reason, considered to be a traffic hazard in Lubbock, Texas. Imagine that.

My job description included no option for me to pursue the panic-stricken bird onto the highway, period. If the chicken was not caught before the end of the parking lot, just strike up a chorus of "Ain't That a Shame" and wave goodbye. While true that the bottom line of Clary Poultry & Egg would be only slightly impacted by the demise of the chicken, the impact on my future would be considerably more significant if I found my way into the traffic. To witness the chaos that ensued when a sightless, brainless chicken darted into the traffic was both frightful and funny.

This book will help you in your work of chasing headless chickens.

Excuse me? You don't chase headless chickens?

Sure you do.

You call them executives, decision-makers, deals, sales, contracts, relationships and strategic contacts. They're actually all headless chickens, and I think you will agree as you read on.

Enjoy the chase!

KNOW YOUR COMPETITION
Even When It's Not Human

I have to tell you that being the backup plan to a one eyed dog was a humbling start in business.

MOST BUSINESSPEOPLE WHO ARE BUILDING THEIR networks and trying to get appointments for themselves or their clients do not spend enough time considering their competition. And by "competition," I am talking in generality rather than a specific person, company or group. Consider the term to encompass everyone else who is trying to get to the same goal.

For me, in those days of chicken chasing, the only competition was Buddy — a one-eyed, herding dog that belonged to Bud, the guy who sent the chickens to the great beyond. Buddy, the dog, was well-known around Clary Poultry & Egg and, before I showed up on the job, was the primary deterrent to a chicken making it to the highway.

Competition can actually make you better at your job. Assuming, of course, that you get an occasional win. Otherwise, it will humiliate and kill you. Most of the time, when you see a Lowe's, across the street will be The Home Depot. They make each other better in every market where they are in close proximity. Having competition nearby to push you to be better at your job is healthy.

Being the backup plan to a one-eyed dog was a humbling start in business. But, the way I look at it more than 50 years later, I am glad this humiliation came so early in my career.

Having some competition forced me to be even more creative, focused and determined.

Being a very observant 9-year-old, I knew Buddy possessed skills I didn't have. For example, Buddy was low to the ground, where the chickens lived, and could turn on a dime. This perspective allowed Buddy to stay focused on the birds that would periodically disappear under the cars in the parking lot. I, on the other hand, was gangly, uncoordinated and slow. This was a fine combination of skills that not only gave Buddy an advantage in chasing chickens but also kept me from being on any of the athletic teams at school.

A second thing working in Buddy's favor was that he was genetically predisposed to chasing and killing birds. Although it would have helped me in this particular job, the bird-chasing gene had been bred out of my bloodline a couple of generations earlier.

Finally, there was a fierce loyalty to his owner that made Buddy the one-eyed, herding dog a formidable competitor. My loyalty to Uncle Art, on the other hand, was slightly lower. To me, it was all about the money. If Uncle Art were not paying me such a handsome fee for this important work, I would have been at home, sitting in front of the window unit air conditioner, staring into the depths of our 50 gallon aquarium or taking things apart. Or perhaps doing all three at the same time.

If I had decided to adapt my gangly frame to Buddy's techniques in order to take away his advantage, I would have hit the ground and run on all fours.

How crazy would that have been?

But that's the way a lot of people and companies operate.

They "cut and paste" strategies and tactics from their competition, and that is never a good solution. They may not fit you or your company's skill sets or culture.

In Rework, Jason Fried and David Heinimeire Hansson write this about competition: "Even if you wind up losing, it's better to go down fighting for what you believe in instead of just imitating others."

Many entrepreneurial endeavors take a competitor's breakthrough and simply make it better. But those that do best are the one's that see a flaw in the competition and create a totally new paradigm. When Reed Hastings received a $40 late fee from a Blockbuster rental, he began putting together the plan for Netflix. There is no question that I would have gone down imitating Buddy and his unique capabilities, so I had to make my being only human work for me.

I had two good eyes and 20/20 vision and specifically, great peripheral vision. I knew that, if I got on the opposite side of Buddy's good eye, it would give me a slight edge in getting a step up on Buddy and an advantage at the start of the pursuit.

It's always good to assess your strengths against your competition's weaknesses no matter what the situation. In this case, 50 cents was at stake every time Buddy and I took off after the same prey.

Another weakness I discovered about my competition was that Buddy was afraid of fast moving cars and wouldn't go all the way to the highway. That bit of knowledge, based on my early observations, told me that if it was an even race to the three-quarter pole, Buddy would come to a sudden stop, and I had 25 feet, with no competition in sight, to catch the bird. You may not think that these two small advantages are important, but it made all the difference in the world in the outcome of the day's totals. If I could just get between Buddy and his prey for a precious few seconds in the red zone, I was the only game in town. In networking and business development, that is exactly where you want to be.

The lesson here, with more to come throughout this book, is to always look for small advantages and leverage points where you can gain some ground on your competition. All of those little things will add up in your favor over time.

Moving from chickens to business, here is an example: A critical advantage over the average competitor is to put your ego aside and understand who really runs your show. Not the show, but your show. I'm talking about the person who controls the access to your executive target, the one who takes their calls, who adds and eliminates people and meetings from their schedules and the one who can either grant you the opportunity of consistent access or make sure you are never heard from again and spend eternity in appointment purgatory. Mainly known as the "executive assistant," these people are the most important people in your network.

Communicating and working with executive assistants has always been a pleasure. They are some of the nicest, smartest and most capable people around. After all, they have figured out how to sit right outside the most luxurious office in the building and work directly with the top people in the corporation. They get to meet important people from outside the company and probably lead a more interesting life than 90 percent of the other frazzled folks in the company who have all kinds of P&L pressures and issues these people have mostly avoided.

Let's assume for a minute that you currently have access to several top-level decision-makers. When is the last time you asked your contact's executive assistant how he or she is doing and if there is any way you can be of assistance?

Chances are the executive assistant will be so dumbstruck with the fact that you are asking the question, she won't be able to think of anything at that moment. But, you asked! Nobody asks! You have just set yourself apart. You have gained the advantage and claimed the high ground in your pursuit of his or her boss. Congratulations.

There are times when the executive cannot attend an event at my invitation, and, if appropriate, I will ask the executive assistant to attend in the executive's place. A few years back $5.00 went a lot further than it does today. A $5.00 Starbucks coupon given to executive assistants for being helpful to my cause was a nice gesture of appreciation. I always sent them after the fact; otherwise they may be seen as a bribe to obtain access to their bosses. It was a "thank you" for their time and efforts. I sent them the coupons even when I didn't get access to their bosses. That really grabbed their attention. I know from the emails and phone calls I received.

Anyone can be rude and demanding and end up getting what he wants. But when the rest of the field is rude and demanding, they are not going to get access through the keeper of the gate.

Be strategic, plant seeds and make deposits in the lives of the people around you, whether or not they can help today or not.

LESSON LEARNED

Don't adapt a "cut and paste" strategy based on someone else's way of pursuing appointments. Be observant and creative in your pursuits.

REVIEW

- Competition can make you better, if you get an occasional win. Always assess and play to your strengths.
- Seek small advantage and leverage points.
- The executive assistant can make or break your effort.

NEVER PLAY OUT OF POSITION

Outcomes largely depend on position.
—Steven S. Little, "The Milkshake Moment"

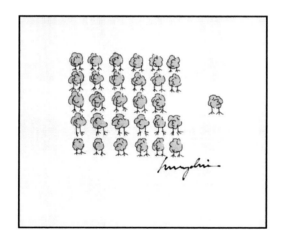

IF YOU'RE GOING TO CHASE HEADLESS CHICKENS THEN you better be out there where the headless chickens are running. They are not going to come to you, because they don't know where you are and because ... well ... they're headless! I never had a chicken jump into my arms on the loading dock — and neither do potential contacts, clients or customers. They are just as "headless" as those chickens when it comes to thinking about you.

And if you think they are going to search for you on the internet and find your website where you extol the wonder of all things you, you are mistaken. In order to meet the people you need to know, you need to spend your time in places where everybody is not just like you. And I'm not talking about a networking gathering sponsored by this or that company or networking-specific organization or the latest hot bar where the up-and-comers all gather for drinks after work, telling business lies and trying to hook-up.

If you were smart enough to pick up this book, you don't really care all that much about the up-and-comers. Let them get together and swarm like bees around the same hive. The level of people you want to meet have moved way past that group; they are the ones who are either your desired contact or someone who can actually help you get where you want to go. You're after the Queen Bee, and you are probably not going to get to her by networking with the worker bees.

Most people at networking events are trying to meet people who can help them. They are trying to meet you, so you can help them get where they want to go. You can spend too many hours at those events and engage in way too many conversations that will result in a pocket full of business cards from nice well-meaning people who are just like you before you read this book! For those of you who follow sports, radio sports guys — you know, the people who have never grown up and have no discernible skills other than criticizing amazing athletes, rude humor and lame personal stories they think are fascinating to all of us — are always talking about people playing out of position. Like they would know. The inference is that when people play out of position, they are not as effective. They have higher risks of injury, and the overall effort of the team suffers. At least that part of what they say makes sense to me. To continue the sports analogy, when you play out of position, your injuries are not the physical kind — unless you slip on an olive, poke your eye out with a drink umbrella or die of boredom at one of those generic networking events. Your injuries are the ones sustained by your network and progress toward the goal of getting appointments with decision-makers and key individuals. Attending generic events where there is no clear focus and no strategy for attendance is definitely playing out of position.

Over the span of your career, plenty of people will come to you for help in the normal course of business. You don't need to go out and find them. And, when they do come, help the one's you can help, and the ones you can't help, connect them with a relationship or a resource that can.

A more strategic alternative to connecting yourself with a key player is to find smaller networking opportunities that are sponsored by a corporation, an industry association, a nonprofit or a university. These are far better opportunities for you than the events that are simply networking events with no real focus and where your success is a long shot at best.

At the sponsored events, at least there will be people in attendance who are high up in the organizations who could be key to your pursuit. In the great book *Superconnect*, Richard Koch and Greg Lockwood, when describing those who are super connectors, write, "More connections, however, are less important than right connections." I couldn't agree more, and you are not likely to find a super connector at an nonsponsored gathering for networking purposes.

You can easily end up as road kill on the business highway simply because you spent too much time with a lot of people who are not interested in helping you achieve your goals. Even if they want to help, chances are they cannot help in a meaningful way. But, you do need to spend a certain percentage of your time helping people and making deposits in their lives with no expectation of a return.

You are not a true giver if every time you give you are expecting something in return. That is an investor, and even though you are making an investment for a return, that should not be your sole purpose. While you are strategically placing yourself in position to meet the right people with every expectation of a return on that investment, you are also looking for opportunities to give without an expectation of return. As you plant the seeds of future success and as you reach out to people to assist others, some of people can and will reciprocate. You can help them through introductions, mentoring, resources or just encouragement.

Here is a strange phenomenon from the animal kingdom that illustrates an interesting way to waste your time. You remember Buddy, the one-eyed, herding dog that was my only competition in the chicken chasing endeavor? Every now and then Buddy would leap up from a lying position and furiously begin chasing his tail. As far as I could tell, this startling act would come out of a deep sleep on the concrete floor of the loading dock. It was a sight to behold, and the absolute last place you wanted to be was in the path of this furry, snarling, snapping cyclone. On two occasions, Buddy threw himself off the loading dock and continued his pursuit of his tail after bouncing off the asphalt parking lot. Talk about focus!

Most vets will tell you that tail chasing is normal in very young dogs. The tail is just another moving object to be investigated, hunted down and sometimes even bitten. But, when older dogs chase their tails, this may be a sign of anxiety, boredom or frustration.

This is a great illustration of the differences between young businesspeople and older more mature businesspeople trying to build a network. As much as I would like to think that Buddy was doing this because his competition, yours truly, was frustrating him. I doubt it.

Here's the analogy ... First there are the young ones chasing the bright shiny objects, running from networking event to networking event and hunting down the objects to the point of exhaustion — lots of energy but mostly misdirected in this tail-chasing exercise and not a lot accomplished at the end of the chase. Then, just like the previous description, there are the older networkers who are a bit anxious and/or frustrated about the fact they are slowing down and falling behind in the technologies and the skills necessary to keep their Rolodex growing. They are bored with it all, frustrated and end up chasing their tails in an entirely different manner or for entirely different reasons. They may have had success in the past that came through involvements in groups and events that are irrelevant today, but they remain involved and refuse to try something new. They may be so risk averse that they will not stray from the comfortable well-worn paths that continually put them with the same people — people just like them.

If you find yourself in either category today, there are ways to redirect that energy and reap the benefits of a strong deep relationship pool that will last a lifetime. They take the form of deposits, which we will discuss later.

LESSON LEARNED

You can easily end up as road kill on the business highway simply because you spent too much time with a lot of people just like you.

REVIEW

- The executive assistant can make or break your effort.
- You must be out where the chickens are running.
- Don't misdirect your energy.
- Be a true giver; don't expect a return from every effort.
- Be strategic about the networking opportunities you choose to attend.

TILTING THE FIELD OF PLAY

If you don't have a competitive advantage, don't compete.
— Jack Welch

THERE IS NO MANUAL FOR CHASING HEADLESS BIRDS. Uncle Art did not show up on the dock when I arrived for my first day and hand me a "Headless Chicken Chasing For Dummies" book. My detailed job instructions came through a cloud of cigar smoke and a gruff, "Figure it out! And just make sure they don't make it to the highway!"

Today, all along the shelves of the Business/Marketing/Sales section of the bookstore and throughout hundreds of web pages of books on Amazon, there are books on how to make a sale once you are in the door. But try to find a good book, in today's gatekeeper environment, on exactly how to get in that door in the first place. You will find all kinds of advice on how to make effective cold calls, letter writing campaigns and super-duper emails that will have the targeted executive drooling over your offer.

Right.

The A-Team combination of email filters, Caller-ID and executive assistants that screen absolutely everything diminish the value of those books. You may get lucky and slip through the cracks or your timing and offer may be perfect. Or not. Sometimes a blind hog does indeed find the acorn.

The truth is, everyday is a new day when you are chasing a headless chicken. What worked yesterday may not work today. You need to develop a dynamic business model that works best for you and your particular skills and personality. I am not going to give you Uncle Art's advice and tell you to "figure it out." This chapter provides insights intended to help you figure it out and take more control of your networking environment.

There is no pattern involved when the bird takes off. There is no videotape to review or PowerPoint to consult, and if there were, it wouldn't help. However, there is always a way to improve any process, and you need to find it quickly through trial, error and attention to the details, and then be careful to not camp out on one solution for too long.

Believing that a singular process will work over a long period of time is not a good idea when chasing appointments with executives. You must keep creating new ways of adapting the process and methods to match the times, the people and situations. Here is a little observation from my chicken chasing days: A headless chicken can run under a 1950s model car at full speed with zero interference. A 9-year-old boy cannot.

Something needed to be done to take the advantage away from my competition other than require Buddy the dog to wear stilts or a top hat. My process had to factor in the occasional disappearance and reappearance of the elusive bird out from under the random automobiles in our field of play — the Clary Poultry & Egg parking lot.

To get a slightly more level playing field, or parking lot in this case, I would convince the two or three guys that worked in that area to park their cars on the same side of the lot, which meant I had to get there early and direct traffic. This

eliminated my competition's multiple disappearances but this only solved part of my problem. The dang bird would still disappear under the cars only now it was out of my reach for a longer period of time. So, in solving one problem, I created another unintended consequence.

This will happen when you have a dynamic business model, thus the "dynamic" part. You must be observant enough to see what went wrong, and change it. In this case, sometimes the critter would reappear even closer to the highway where the chase had to end! Not good.

I discovered that if I strategically positioned one of the old damaged chicken crates next to the car closest to the dock, the chicken could not disappear under that car but rather would careen off the crate and back onto the field of play. Problem solved. At that point, it was up to me to play the angle of the careening chicken to my advantage. It was sort of like playing billiards with chickens.

The great Wayne Gretzky said, "Skate to where the puck is going, not to where it is." It is always useful when estimating the future position of a careening headless bird, as it is in networking, to position yourself where the action and the opportunity will be. Future tense.

You can control the environment in small ways if you are creative, quickly learn from your mistakes and anticipate. What about the playing field of a large event you are attending where there are several people you need to meet? If you can get your hands on the list of attendees beforehand, you have just dramatically altered the playing field in your favor. Knowing who is going to be there can even save you some money and time. If there is no one on that list you want to meet, then reconsider your involvement. Although it's not necessarily easy to acquire the attendee list to most events, it can be done. Sometimes the list of attendees is posted in the invitations that are issued on the internet via email when they request an RSVP. The invitation will also allow you to view the entire guest list or at least who has responded by hitting the "yes" button. Also, on rare occasions, there will be the entire invitation list and their emails at the top of the email. That is pure networking gold.

Another method of acquiring such a list from an event is to call the organizers of the event and volunteer your services. I've done this many times for several reasons. First, I genuinely wanted to contribute to the success of the event by helping and, as a result, be thought of as someone who is a giver. Also, I wanted to know who was attending the event (the elusive list) and finally, I wanted to be in position to meet the speaker before the meeting or without standing in a long line at the conclusion of the event.

Several times I was asked if I would work the check-in table. Bingo! I couldn't have asked for a better spot to put names with faces and say a few words to the people I specifically wanted to meet. I would even ask them for permission to spend a minute or two with them later. I was rarely turned down in this request. Why? Partly because they saw me serving others and that is a great place to be seen.

Doing this was helpful in a couple of ways. It was a help to the organizers to have another person to fill a position. It was helpful to me in getting familiarized with the attendees and, on one occasion, they invited me to sit at the table with their company that was positioned right in front of the speaker's podium. A trifecta any way you look at it. These actions all tilt the field of play in your favor.

At the poultry plant there was a bulletin board in the break room with pictures of people who had been there the longest and had achieved some degree of poultry stardom. Even as a little kid I made it my business to take note of the "heavy-hitters" around the place and would sit at their table at lunch. Never hurts to be in the know about all things poultry.

Let's assume you have followed this advice and now have the list in your possession. If you have access to the internet, you can do a considerable amount of research, including finding a photograph of the people you want to meet. In the past, I've actually copied photographs to my smartphone so I have it available when I attend the event. I've snapped pictures with my phone of executives in the newspaper and local magazines when they are featured in articles or receive promotions and keep them in a folder in the photo section of the phone with notes.

How many times have you been to an event or trade show and you knew the name of the person you wanted to meet but had no idea what they looked like? You spent all of your time circling little groups of people, craning your neck and squinting your eyes trying to read name tags while the two of you are in motion? What a beating.

Suffice it to say there is no reason you should ever show up at an event to meet specific people and not know what they look like. Find some photos on LinkedIn, Facebook, the "About Us" or "Company" pages of the website, and put them to use. You should also be able to see the board members of the sponsoring company on the "Investor" page if they are a public company or the "About Us" page if they are privately held. Finally, the ability to Google someone on a phone's browser during an event to learn something about an executive is priceless.

I have been across from executives at a table and have researched them on my phone to learn the latest news about their company or any other fact that would open a conversation. I learned to do that by looking at the pictures on that lunchroom bulletin board. I have also visually scanned the array of name tags usually displayed on the table at the entrance of an event and then did "on the fly" research on the names that looked interesting based on their company and titles. Several times I have taken a photograph of the array of name tags and gone off to a quiet place to take stock of the attendees. This is not rocket science. This is just good R&D

as part of an overall strategy. About all I had to go on at the chicken coop was the employees embroidered pocket patch with their names proudly displayed.

At nonprofit events, before you volunteer to help with the event, do the same kind of research you performed on the corporate executives, but this time do it on the board members of the nonprofit. These organizations are proud of the hoity-toity folks that sit on their board and will usually publish a short bio on them. They should be proud of these board members because these are generally the best and brightest and most accomplished people available. The very fact that they are actively participating on a nonprofit board is a good indication they are givers. These are people you can learn from in your own journey toward being a giver. Meet these people, ask well-informed questions about their involvement in the organization and let them know you are interested in helping.

Once again, if you go to their news or events pages of their websites you will probably find past events with photos posted of the very people you would like to meet. When you have the information and have cut and pasted a photo into your phone, look for a reason to introduce yourself to any of them in attendance at the event. That could be in the form of a mutual friend, a mutual interest, alumni association or any number of things you can gather from your research. Who knows when you will be driving nails for Habitat For Humanity and be next to someone who could be a key to your future success? You better know who they are, what they look like, where they went to school and as much information as you can legally acquire. This will enable you to engage in a conversation that is both comfortable and productive. The absolute last thing you want to do is to engage in a conversation with an executive and have that person walk away thinking it was a waste of time.

Another goldmine of information, which can help you make the connections you need, is the annual report of a public company that can be downloaded from their website. This report is usually found on the "Investor" page. The 10K & 10Q filings of the annual and quarterly reports will provide information related to competition, market risk, executives, etc. In particular, none of this information may be important, but overall it gives you a view of the company that could be useful.

You will find a wealth of conversation-starting information on public companies in the presentations they make to the investment bankers, at their industry conventions or local meetings. This is also found on the "Investor" page of the website. After learning the facts outlined in these presentations, you will get at least an overview of their strategy and how the product or service you offer might help. When you take advantage of the free information that is available to you, you have just significantly altered the landscape in your favor.

None of these recommendations are devious, underhanded or in any way clandestine. This is just good R&D like any smart company would do as it pursues clients or customers. Think of it as the same kind of research a good investor would do before making a financial investment or a good employer would do when making a critical hiring decision. I seriously doubt Uncle Art had me checked out before making me the job offer but who knows? Maybe he checked the dreaded "permanent record" at my school. The investment you are considering is an investment of your time but is equally important as a financial investment if not more so. Your money can be replaced, your time cannot.

Nobody ever said you have to be a big company to have an R&D department. It's you, in a coffee shop, the internet and your laptop just like it was me, in the lunchroom and some pocket-sized photos — same concept just a little less technical. So, get out there and research, develop and drink those double whatever lattes!

Continually expand and improve your process. Nobody's going to do it for you. If your network is going to increase in value for you and your clients it better increase in the quality of the people you meet. If you don't do your research, you run the risk of growing your network in size and scope but not in quality. That is a formula for mediocrity.

When your R&D department has defined where you need to go and with whom you need to meet, and you have made initial contact through application of the methods we have already discussed, the next thing you need to consider is how to make it easy for people to do business with you. On a personal level, if you are my dry cleaner, my grocer, my bank or my gym, make it easy for me to do business with you, and I'll be back. Even if you do a good job technically, if it difficult to do business with you and your product or service is equal to your competitors, I will take the easier path. If you have the option, life is too short to deal with difficult people.

One of the best ways to start off a relationship in business, or anywhere else for that matter, is to ask the question, "How do you like to communicate?" Obviously, I didn't have the opportunity to do this with the headless chickens, but you can ask the question to just about anyone you meet if you believe that there will be ongoing dialogue. If you are always shooting an email to someone who prefers a phone call, you are slowing down the progress of the relationship. Or, if you are placing phone calls and they don't check their voicemail but once a decade because they prefer email, you are toast. You think they are ignoring your request or are being just plain rude when in reality they have no idea you are trying to reach them.

This is such a simple thing, yet I cannot recall anyone ever asking me the question, "Trent, how do you prefer that I communicate with you?" Just asking the question, you are saying to that person that you value their time enough to ask this simple but important question. Then, when you have that information, you can communicate the way they want to communicate. That simple act puts you in the category of someone who is thoughtful in the way you relate and do business with people. Exactly the place you want to be.

The dock foreman at Clary Poultry & Egg was very hard of hearing and too vain to wear a hearing aid. If you wanted something from him, you literally had to get in front of him so he knew you needed his attention. Everyone seemed to know that except me, and it severely hampered my communication with Chuck. When I learned about this requirement, life got a whole lot easier on the dock. After you have asked them how they like to communicate, you need to remember it. Put it in the notes section of their information wherever you keep your contact database.

I asked this question to the CFO of a $9 billion company where I had introduced my client and had found a great piece of business. He said, "Always mark your emails to me

'Urgent' because those are the only ones I open." Wow! What an incredibly important piece of information that turned out to be as we moved forward in our relationship. What if I had not asked that question? My client and I could have spent a lifetime in email purgatory trying to communicate with an executive who was key to the success of the engagement. These are personal preferences, and you need to know them.

Another small point of leverage to separate you from the pack and tilt the field in your favor is to follow up an initial meeting quickly, in a creative and thoughtful way. Believe me when I say that nothing shouts, "I don't care" like a brief follow-up email to an initial meeting with an important prospect or connection. The exception to that statement is if they have specifically asked for something that needs to be sent quickly and there is no better way to fulfill their request than email. That request could take the form of an article, a presentation or a link that takes advantage of email as the best option for a communication tool. My alternative to the "quick response" is to take out a real piece of paper and a real pen (a fountain pen if you really want to make an impression) and write a real note. Then put it in a real envelope with a real stamp, and put it in a real mailbox. Your chances of getting a real response will increase tenfold. Really.

Just about everyone on the planet sends quick emails. If you met the person at a larger gathering where, there is a good chance your competitor also made her acquaintance, this action item becomes even more important. Let her get a quick and absolutely meaningless email from your competitor and a thoughtfully hand-written note from you. See which one she remembers and who gets the best response. My money is on you. And if she receives your note within 48 hours of the meeting or phone call, that's even better.

When I travel and have preset appointments with individuals, I pre-address and stamp envelopes to each one and take along blank cards for the follow-up notes. Then, if at all possible, I mail them before I leave town. Just drop them off at the hotel desk, and they will do the rest. This is so simple, yet so effective.

If you are thinking at this point that your handwriting is terrible and looks like "hen scratching," then use your computer to print out your message and personally sign the note with a real fountain pen instead of the ballpoint that you found at the gas station. Yes, that will take a little more time, but remember the goal is to differentiate yourself and tilt the field to your advantage. Something as small as the difference between a ballpoint and a fountain pen is just one more thoughtful and tasteful action that will set you apart from everyone else.

One more comment regarding the written notes … When you are following up on a meeting you've had in your local area, drop the note by the front desk of their office if possible. On more than one occasion I have run into executives in the hallway or the lobby of their offices. Handing them the note and having a brief conversation was priceless. I guarantee that if you take the time and go to the expense of writing a handwritten note on a nice card, putting it in a matching envelope and mailing it with a real stamp, it will never get caught in a filter. It will set you apart immediately as someone who is more concerned about being effective in business relationships than simply being efficient.

Just like the bulletin board was the main source of communication back in 1953, writing notes and letters, posting them and putting them in the mail was the best way to communicate. That practice began to slip into obscurity about 10 or 15 years ago. Today, with email, voicemail, texting and Twitter, this seemingly archaic method of communication is deemed completely inefficient. That's right. It is inefficient. But efficiency is not going to tilt the field of play as much as being effective.

A few paragraphs ago I told you to ask them how they like to communicate, and then I immediately told you to take the initiative to send a handwritten note. Those two statements may seem at odds with each other. My suggestion is that you send the note after the initial meeting and, after that, communicate as they requested.

One last suggestion of differentiation is to buy a Mont Blanc or some other nice writing instrument and carry it in your shirt pocket. It speaks of stability, quality and professionalism. This is assuming that you are trying to run with the big boys and girls rather trying to meet someone who can get you a good deal on auto repairs. In that case a BIC will do. And, when you are buying dress shirts, buy shirts with a pocket. Otherwise, don't bother buying an expensive pen. And, you will have a place for your clip-on name tag holder if you are not wearing a jacket. Otherwise, it will be sideways clipped to your shirt opening or on your pants pocket. Smooth.

In summary, it's all about gaining a competitive advantage through the initial impact you can have in communication styles, differentiating yourself and establishing a presence that is memorable. My shouting or Buddy's barking didn't make a difference to the headless chickens, but the way you communicate with the decision-makers will make a big difference in the success of your pursuits.

On one occasion I needed to get in front of the CEO of an $850 million corporation for three of my clients. In a flash of what some would call brilliance and others would call insanity, I quickly wrote on the back of a Corner Bakery brown napkin this note: "Eric, I would like to talk to you about three of my clients (and then listed them), and it will take about 10 minutes for each. I believe there is value in each of them, and it will be time well spent." I put it into an envelope and mailed it. Less than a week later I received a call from his assistant offering times that he could meet with me. When I walked into his office, he stood, picked up the napkin from his desk and put it between us on the small conference table. We had a discussion about all three companies. He was gracious, as I've come to know him to be in every situation, and he was generous with his guidance and contacts. When we finished talking about my clients, I asked him what he thought about my using the napkin as a way to communicate. His smiling response was, "You're sitting here aren't you?"

I'm not suggesting that you copy my methods. The fact is, that was about three years ago, and I have never done it again. It was random; it was out of the box; and it served the purpose of differentiating me from others who were vying for 30 minutes of time with a very busy man.

You need to consider having a backup plan. Uncle Art had a backup plan. His first plan was a one-eyed dog that came free with the chicken executioner. His backup plan was to hire his wife's sister's kid for next to nothing, promising her he wouldn't get on the highway. Your backup plan should be a little more strategic than Uncle Art's.

There will be many instances in which you simply cannot get to the contact under the power of your own efforts. Sometimes you will need to get help and triangulate the effort. In other words … sometimes you may need help from another headless chicken chaser. There were actually times that another worker would, just for the fun of it, assist me in the chase. Don't let your ego get in the way by trying to do it all yourself. You can depend on people you trust not to poach your chicken, and you can leverage outside influences to meet your goal.

Sometimes Buddy, when he ran into the frightened feather duster, would actually herd it right into my hands. His bark didn't do any good because, of course, the chicken had no head and, therefore, no ears. Not that they actually have ears. They don't. That's why you never see a chicken wearing glasses. Sometimes people very close to you can bring their influence to bear on a situation and shorten your chase.

If you do engage others to help you catch the headless chicken, share some of the spoils with them if you make a deal. There was an old saying I used to hear in the manufacturer rep business when someone would ask, "How's business?" The answer would come, "Some days chicken, some days feathers." Make sure you share the chicken with those who give you help and, when the chase results in feathers, just keep those to yourself.

I don't remember having to split my per-chicken reward with any of my fellow workers but, if your chase involves a direct financial reward in the form of a fee or commission from your client, be ready to share with the one who was directly responsible for your success.

LESSON LEARNED

Believing a singular process will work over a long period of time is not a good idea when chasing appointments with busy executives.

REVIEW

- Always seek to take control of your networking environment.
- Research, research, research.
- Execute, execute, execute.

BE FLEXIBLE, AND HAVE TWO MAPS

Stay committed to your decisions, but stay flexible in your approach.
—Tony Robbins

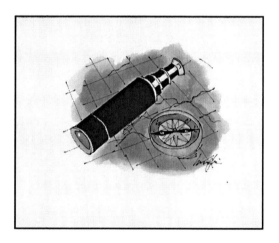

THE WHOLE WORLD OF NETWORKING, EITHER FOR business or for life, is somewhat like a "connect the dots" game you see on the children's menus at breakfast restaurants and diners. On the menu you will find a random bunch of dots with numbers beside them, and the goal is to connect the dots with lines until the picture appears. This is a wonderful distraction for an antsy child while the food is being prepared and a nice illustration for our purposes. By the way, a big "thank you" to every restaurant that provides these wonderful anti-stress solutions for parents.

The difference between those games and the real-world puzzle of networking with a strategic purpose is that there are no numbers next to the dots and the picture will take on new shapes halfway through the process. Or, in the middle of the process of connecting what you believe are the correct dots, the next dot will disappear and there is suddenly no connection between where you are and where you need to be. This makes flexibility, creativity and adaptation to change a critical advantage as you pursue the headless chickens.

Headless chickens can and will change directions with alarming frequency. The shifting marketplace mentioned in the previous chapter is the parking lot where we play. Your ability and willingness to change course, when the target moves in an unexpected direction, is key to your success. There is no long-term plan when it comes to chasing chickens. But there better be a short-term plan. Make it a very short and very flexible plan.

In the great book, Rework, Jason Fried and David Heinemeier explain: "If you keep your mass low, you can quickly change anything: your entire business model, product, feature set, and/or marketing message. You can make mistakes and fix them quickly. You can change your priorities, product mix or focus. And most importantly, you can change your mind."

I realize they are referring to the size of a company in that statement, but the same thing applies in any pursuit. Big companies are anything but flexible. As an individual, you get big and equally inflexible when you take on too many pursuits at one time or you are too rigid in your thinking and especially in your routines. You also add to your mass when you spend big bucks on branding and marketing materials that cannot be easily changed.

A 9-year-old kid only knows one thing, and that thing is go as hard as you can as long as you can because every day it all ends at five o'clock. Dinner, a bath, homework and eight or 10 hours of sleep and then it starts all over again. For me, it was basically Groundhog Day every day at the chicken plant. If you haven't seen the 1993 Bill Murray movie Groundhog Day, rent it, and enjoy how he evolves from a selfish prig into a caring individual when he discovers he can actually help people and, in the process, impact his own life in a positive way. So can you.

We've already discussed tilting the field of play in your favor with things you learn about the players. In business, especially when it all depends on you, the tendency is to think like that 9-year-old boy and just go flat out all the time. The reality is that each day compounds itself upon the other, and if you are not fit for the chase or you have made too many commitments, you will never catch the headless chickens. If you are high on the attention deficit scale, this will always be an uphill battle for you. I've been there. I am there.

Now, where was I?

Oh yes, that doesn't really go away so you just have to channel that combination of energy, curiosity and short attention span to your advantage. I decided early on that instead of medication I would choose dedication to overcome that perceived weakness.

We've said before that speed is important, but pace is also important when chasing headless chickens and when chasing busy decision-makers. This is yet another seemingly contradictory statement. While the pace of the executive is important, your pace is even more critical.

Here is a quick point of clarification before we go on ... Speed to the target is vital, and when you do get close to the opportunity, the very last thing you want to do is force your way into that opportunity or onto that person. Even though you might consider getting the appointment or the deal to be a success, in the process you may have alienated all of the players involved. Technically it is a win. You got the appointment. You closed the deal. Try it again with the same group, and I bet you are shut out. Pace the chase. Don't go flat out all of the time. Don't force the issue. Don't just finish; finish well.

There is a right way and a wrong way to get to success in the building of a network and getting the critical appointments you need for yourself or for a client.

When we were raising our two girls, my wife was the black and white straight-line thinker who read all of the books on child rearing and wanted them to follow that exact course to adulthood. I, on the other hand, was the relationship-driven loop thinker who was always more concerned that we maintained a great relationship with the girls than that they did everything exactly according to the book and on the correct timeline. If Pam had written this book, it would be very informative, it would not be funny and it would probably be a great trifold brochure. On the other hand, if I had raised our girls by myself, they would be a mess but would love me a great deal. By the grace of God, they are wonderful young women who have made great decisions in their lives and are passing that pattern on to their children. And, we have a great relationship with them and their families. Mission accomplished.

The point is that there will always be guidelines and bullet pointed presentations on how to network, and you may have followed them to a tee and have it all figured out. But every plan needs to be open to change with the bottom line being to get to the goal in a manner and with a style that preserves relationships and leaves doors open for future connections. I read once that, "A map always tells you everything except how to refold it."

When I was chasing headless chickens, there were no manuals, no mentoring programs and no tools available to make the chase more successful. There was the chicken, the parking lot and yours truly. About the only other vital tool was a pair of sneakers with a little remaining tread. There certainly was nothing like a map that would tell me where the chicken was going to be. However, in the business world, there are tools that can be extremely useful in helping you with your chase. Mapping your relationships is important. In relationships, where you've been is just as important as where you're going. Looking backward you are keeping track of the people who helped you get where you are today. That's important for a couple of reasons.

The older you get and the busier you get, the more forgetful you are about the people who introduced you to the person who introduced you to the person who actually made something good happen — either in business or just your life in general. You may be four or five people or several months or years removed from the introduction by the time something comes of that initial contact. The busier you get, the less time you have to figure it out and track backward to those contacts who linked you to the successful ending. Here's why this is important ...

People really appreciate the fact that you took the time to let them know what happened as a result of that introduction — whether it was a week ago or a year ago. This just doesn't happen in today's world. You are doing something that is out of the ordinary and something you should do just as a good human being. The action of reaching back and communicating the results reestablishes the connection with that person in a way that is memorable, and it communicates genuine appreciation for the time he or she took to help. Also, it will move you to a top-of-mind position with that person and when there are other people she thinks you should meet or someone she knows who could help, or, which is often the case, that you could help, she will call. But, whichever happens, you're back in position to receive that call or email. "Out of sight, out of mind?" Not any more. Always be reaching back to the degree that it makes sense. It will pay dividends for a long time.

I use an application on my iPhone and iPad called MindMap Pro. It allows me to quickly create visual maps of introductions, add notes to those maps that tell me where that contact came from and I can go to it in the middle of any situation and figure out where I am on the relationship road. I don't get lost. I know exactly where I've been, where I am and where I'm going. I used to just draw circles around names and lines connecting those circled names to other names. Even though I still start there from time to time, I now have a technology that keeps those maps on all devices. That way, if I run in to someone who is on one of those maps, I can do some quick research, see the relationship chain and give them an update on other people up or down that chain.

I also use an application called Evernote to photograph business cards as I get them, and I put a comment in the notes section regarding where I was and the person who made the introduction or created the opportunity.

So the mix of old school high-touch with present day high-tech is a good combination for success in building a network that reaches back to recognize those who have helped in the past and reaching forward to those who may help in the future.

LESSONS LEARNED

In relationships, where you've been is just as important as where you are going.

REVIEW

- Be fit for the pursuit by taking care of yourself first.
- Get appointments the right way, not just any way.
- Always have two dynamic maps working.
- Reach back and communicate with those who have helped.

TRUST & MAKING DEPOSITS

*The best things in life are earned by making daily deposits into the "effort account"
needed to achieve it.*
—Tom Ziglar

IN THE LATE 70S, I USED TO ROAM THE SIDELINES OF VERY exciting 8-year-old girls' soccer games when Tom Ziglar, son of the late and great Zig Ziglar, was my youngest daughter's coach. What was going on between the lines was not nearly as interesting as what was taking place on the sidelines of those games. Zig and I would chat about various things, and then he would excuse himself and walk about 20 feet away and begin talking into a small recorder.

Zig, in his maroon jogging suit, would do this over and over and over during every game. Curiosity finally got the best of me, and I asked what the heck he was recording. He said, "Observations, stories tied to those observations and principles tied to both." Zig was a master storyteller, and these recordings were the genesis of those principle-based stories in books, videos and live presentations for decades. But he was also recording notes to himself about checking in on people, following up on promises he'd made and reminders about thank you notes that needed to be written.

I know that because he wouldn't walk away to record those notes. Zig, on the sidelines of a children's soccer game, was starting the process of making deposits in people's lives and building trust through his kindness and consistency. It was as natural to him as breathing. With practice, it can be the same with you. I recommend that you look for his books and load up on his wisdom.

The theme of making deposits into people's lives is common throughout this book, and because it is so vitally important to your life and the lives of the people around you, we are going to expand the conversation into the area of trust. Very simply put, if you make deposits, you are building trust. If you break the trust, it is a withdrawal from that trust account. For the purpose of our discussion, there are three kinds of trust:

1. Earned trust
2. Transferred trust
3. Broken trust

Earned trust may begin with small actions on your behalf that have the accumulative effect of deposits made to an account. This process of building trust takes time, and it involves the steady practice of making these deposits into individuals or businesses. Think of it like a water well that took a very long time to dig and from which you intend to drink for the rest of your life. As people watch and evaluate you on the basis of the deposits you make, your consistency and delivering on your word, the trust grows and the well gets deeper. Work hard as you build trust, but work even harder to ensure that you don't damage trust that has been established. It only takes a few small drops of poison to contaminate a perfectly good well. The same is true with a good network.

The second kind of trust is transferred trust. Earning trust and breaking trust are straightforward acts of continual addition and subtraction. Deposits and withdrawals can be single acts that are mostly transactional in nature. Transferred trust is a more complicated issue than earned or broken trust. Something is set in motion when someone introduces a trusted relationship to you. There is, for lack of a better description, a handoff of a valuable asset, and your responsibility at that point is to honor that relationship and do your best to not violate any aspect of that trust. The transfer of trust comes in the form of an action that takes place — an introductory email, phone call, written note or, best of all, a personal face-to-face introduction. It can also come in the form of a recommendation where there is a product or service involved such as a mechanic or insurance agent. In this discussion, the transfer of trust takes the form of a person-to-person introduction.

While earning and breaking trust are more transactional in nature, transferring trust is something that a person puts into action with an introduction, and then they relinquish control of where it goes from there, which is precisely why it is called "trust." They trust that what they have set in motion will achieve a purpose that would not have been served had that introduction not been made. When you are the recipient of someone's trust in an introduction, the burden of responsibility to treat both people involved with the utmost respect is critical. Make them happy they trusted you, and they might do it again — and again and again.

That brings us to the third kind of trust and that is broken trust. Trust, earned over time, can be broken in a single event or action. When trust is broken, it can take much longer to repair than it did to build. Break the trust and not only will you damage your chances of regaining the momentum with that

individual but you will also run the risk of the word spreading like poison in his or her network. No matter how deep the well, it doesn't take much poison to make it worthless or at least worth less.

There are three basic actions to remember as you network and build trust with people: show up, stand up and follow up.

First you must show up. George L. Bell said, "You can pretend to care, but you can't pretend to show up." When you enter a contest it's usually stated in the rules that, "You must be present to win." Or perhaps it reads, "Not necessary to be present to win." These are two very different rules, and if you are trying to win a chain saw at the True Value Hardware Store, either one could apply. However, if you are trying to build winning relationships, for that to be successful, you must be present to win. You must show up.

By "showing up," I mean giving your full attention to the relationship building blocks of your personal and professional network. This is not something you consign to your executive assistant or pursue with the casual attitude of: "Well, if this networking thing works out that will be great." It's absolutely not a LinkedIn exercise. Nothing replaces face-to-face conversations. That is where I am at my best.

Last year, in an attempt to take my personal network to a new level, I had more than 120 new face-to-face meetings with people I had never met before. This was not a frantic attempt to see how many new people I could meet but rather a strategic use of my time and my current connections to both broaden and deepen my Rolodex. Sometimes you will have time to do that and other times you won't. Just take advantage of the time that becomes available. In the lulls between the chasing of headless chickens, I would make it my business to see what other things were taking place on the loading docks. When my big promotion came, assembling corrugated metal grain storage silos at the other end of the dock, I was already familiar with the people and the process.

Most of those 120 interactions were spent looking people in the eye and giving them the feeling that they are the most important person in my world at that moment. These meetings were variable in length and intensity. Your interactions don't have to be hour-long meetings to be effective in starting the process of building trust. Most of the time you begin the new relationship on the foundation of the transferred trust from a third party.

I am not a big phone talker but that is the second best option when you are getting to know someone. Email is the third and weakest option. Granted, getting a meeting may require a few emails and a couple of phone calls to make that happen, but when you are finally there, be all there. Give the person your full attention. Show up. Leave the phone in the car. (Gasp!) Just turning off the ringer and setting it on "buzz" is not the answer. Or, if the thought of leaving it in the car sends you into orbit, put it in your backpack or briefcase.

When I am in a meeting, whether it is in a boardroom or a coffee shop, I take genuine offense if the other person continually grabs for his phone when it vibrates like it's some kind of grenade that must be prevented from exploding.

One more point ... When asking for a face-to-face meeting with a decision-maker, ask for 20 minutes, and if things go well, it will always extend to 30 minutes or more. If you cannot get your point across in 20 minutes, you are sunk anyway. And when you are in the meeting with the person, ask probing questions that hit the person's hot buttons and then stand back and listen.

Jason Fried wrote the best quote that relates to standing up in his book, Rework: "What you do matters, not what you think, say or plan." Standing up means that you need to do your absolute best to be a person of your word as you endeavor to build these trusted relationships. Become known as someone who is not only a giver much more than a taker, but also someone who makes good on commitments. When you are leaving a meeting, don't just casually say to someone, "I'll give you a call," if you do not have every intention of making that call in a reasonable timeframe. And, unless you fall into a coma over the next week or two, follow through on the commitment to call. When you make that call, if you get a voicemail or talk to an executive assistant, reiterate that this is the call you promised at a previous meeting and leave the appropriate message with some kind of suggested action at the end of the call. The fact that you were in a meeting with this person's boss gives you some degree of credibility. Certainly one of the actions you should request is a return call, but you might also consider asking permission to call again at some scheduled time determined by the executive assistant. Done. Promise fulfilled.

One small deposit made and a follow-up action is requested. If you promise to send the person something as a follow up, then do it! The person may actually forget that you made that promise. But you can't take that chance. And, if he or she did forget, the follow-up call or the arrival of that "something" in the mail will be both impressive and bring you back to the forefront of his or mind. Just this week, after mentioning a book to a new acquaintance at lunch, I made my way to a Barnes & Noble in the area and hand-delivered the book with a note the next day.

When you do get a meeting with someone, show up a few minutes before the time you have arranged to meet. This is such a basic rule of etiquette that I shouldn't have to mention it here. But I am mentioning it because not showing up on time is a show of complete disregard for the other person's time, and it is an act that puts you and your perceived importance above theirs. This is a huge deduction of trust!

Leave early. Arrive early.

If you are late to the first encounter, you have just cast yourself in a negative light. This is not the way to start a relationship — in professional or personal life. If you have a legitimate excuse for being late, call the person and let him off the hook for the meeting, or ask if he can accommodate your late arrival without it impacting the rest of his day. Once again, turn a negative that you created into a small positive with your admission of failure, and this simple request for a follow-up action.

Following is an example of a positive twist on being late or completely missing a meeting when you are the one who is on the receiving end of the missed appointment.

Throughout my career as a manufacturer's representative and building Benchmark Sales over a 16-year period, I never became angry about being stood up for a meeting or someone being late. Here's why ... By being gracious about the missed meeting or the person's tardiness, I put myself in a positive position in this new relationship. And that's where you want to be. In a quirky way, that is a deposit. Be gracious when it happens to you. You may need that deposit someday if you are on the other side of that missed appointment.

The final thing I would say about showing up is, please don't take meetings with a total "What's in this for me" attitude. Certainly you are hopeful that the meeting will be a good use of your time and help you in some way. But, if you will come with the welfare of the others in mind, you will get more and more invitations and opportunities to meet and be introduced into their networks. Remember, you are attempting to build trust and this is just one more way to accomplish that goal.

Come with information that is valuable to the person(s) with whom you are meeting. Do your homework on the subject of the meeting and the people involved so you add value to the meeting. Google them, go to LinkedIn to see what organizations they are involved in outside of business and do some research on the work of that group. Check their business bio on their company website.

Finally, be consistent in your dealings with people so you will always be thought of as a person who is prepared, helpful and, above all, thoughtful. A great quote (unknown author) to keep in mind is: "People with good intentions make promises. People with good character keep them."

In summary, by standing, you convey the fact that you will do what you said you will do. By following up, solidify the fact that you have done what you said you would do. I told Uncle Art that I would do my best to make sure no chickens made it to Highway 82 with or without heads. He expected my best effort, and that's what he got. Maybe that's why I got the big promotion later and moved up to building storage tanks in the sweltering heat. Yes sir. I was livin' the dream.

I cannot emphasize enough the importance of following up when networking and building relationships. But, for right now, suffice it to say that if you are not good at follow up you will build a reputation that will limit your chances of success no matter what you do in life.

If you don't follow up on your commitments, people will limit your access to their trusted relationships and to their resources. Maybe you promised them a connection, a name, a resource or something as simple as a phone number or email address that will help their cause. No matter how simple the commitment, it is essential that you follow up on that promise.

There have been times I could not deliver on a commitment due to circumstances that were out of my control. That's OK. The main thing is that you make the effort, and then report the result back to the person. Even when you fail to deliver, people appreciate the effort you have made on their behalf. You have just made a deposit even when you didn't completely deliver. Simply having asked the question, "What can I do for you" and then making a genuine effort to deliver is a deposit.

One of the shallow substitutes for showing up is the internet and social media. Acts that used to be considered important in building trusted relationships are being slowly replaced by doing things like accepting a LinkedIn invitation to connect and bingo the person is now considered a colleague, friend or one of several more categories. Really? And if none of the seven or eight categories exactly describes the person's relationship to you there is an "other" category. How unimportant do you have to be to fall into the "other" category?

If you are accepting any and all invitations just so your social media profile will be more impressive, stop wasting your time. Believe it or not, people will cruise through your connections on LinkedIn and make judgments about you based on your connections. Keep it on slow growth mode and you might even prune it from time-to-time to keep it in a manageable, and believable, range. LinkedIn is a great tool when used properly but don't make it a substitute for showing up and doing the work of establishing personal connections.

When people say they "know" someone, I drop that into several possible categories of "knowing." At the bottom of the list is that they know who the person is and maybe they were in the same room at an event. Next would be that they had an introduction to the person in a small group. A little closer to the top of my list would be that the person actually knows who they are and would recognize their name. At the top of the list is that the person they "know" would return their phone call. That kind of "knowing" someone in the world of complex networking and relationships is nirvana.

We have already stated that the trust you have earned over time can be broken in a single event or action and can take longer to repair than it did to build. If you do get out of position, and begin to make promises you cannot keep, or if you play one person against another, trying to get what you want, word will travel quickly and you could become known as untrustworthy.

A lack of trust is the kiss of death when building a network and chasing appointments, deals and opportunities. In this day and time, with all of the instant methods of communication that are available, bad news travels fast. When you apply the "Six Degrees of Separation" equation and the lightning speed of Twitter, bad news doesn't have to travel very far to be devastating to the various levels of trust you have worked hard to build.

The building of the relationship capital necessary to network successfully depends largely on your making a lot more deposits in the lives of people than withdrawals. If you try to make the withdrawals before making the necessary deposits, you will experience "arrested development." When people see you coming toward them, they either see you as a "giver" or a "taker" based on their dealings with you in the past and/or what they have heard from mutual acquaintances. You always want to be seen on the positive side of that ledger.

LESSON LEARNED

A lack of trust is the kiss of death when building a network. With the aid of today's communications, bad news will travel fast.

REVIEW

- You must be present to win.
- Do your homework and never be late.
- Show up, stand up and follow up.
- Make people happy they chose to trust you.

MENTORING AND RELATIONSHIP CAPITAL

We make a living by what we get; we make a life by what we give.
—Winston Churchill

THERE WAS NO OFFICIAL MENTORING PROGRAM AT Clary Poultry & Egg. The only one at the plant that had any experience in chasing headless chickens was, unfortunately, not human and therefore was limited in passing along useful information.

I am a strong believer in being involved in a mentoring process — both giving and receiving mentoring — no matter where you are in your life's journey. The Southern Methodist University Cox School of Business in Dallas has a wonderful Associate Board that offers mentoring opportunities to full-time students of the MBA, Professional MBA and Executive MBA programs. The Associate Board program was founded more than 35 years ago by one of my mentors, Dr. Bobby Lyle for which the Southern Methodist University Lyle School of Engineering is named. During most Associate Board meetings, early in the mentoring relationship, the conversation quickly turns to: "How do I build the kind of relationships that will be beneficial from a career perspective?" After doing this for about 15 years, I found the best way to answer that question is, "Do you see that bank across the street? (And please believe me, in Dallas, Texas, there is always a bank across the street from where I meet anyone). I then ask them, "Do you have money in that bank across the street? Because, if you don't, and you go into that bank and demand that they give you money, that's called 'robbery' and, not only will you not get any money, you will probably be arrested."

It is the same with relationships.

There are all kinds of capital in this world — financial capital, emotional capital and relationship capital. Relationship capital is the kind of capital that is deposited and withdrawn over time. And just like your financial bank account, there is always a balance in the account, either positive or negative from where you opened that particular account. If you have not made the necessary deposits, and you try to make a withdrawal that is over the balance, you will have failed in your attempt to get to your goal. With relationship capital, it's just like robbing the bank and getting caught but without the actual jail time. However, if you don't pay careful attention to the balance with each individual and group, you can put yourself in "relationship jail" with those people or groups and end up serving a long and unfruitful sentence.

When we start this conversation, most of the students have no clue what I mean by deposits and withdrawals or exactly how or where you make them. And you can only take the bank analogy so far without coming up with real-world examples of how it's done. I tell them the easiest and best place to start is by making deposits into the people who are immediately around them. In the case of the MBA students, it is their fellow classmates. Those men and women are going to go on to be leaders in the business community and letting this opportunity pass would be a real waste. The professors and guest speakers in the classrooms are the next easiest group to engage in conversations that could lead to long-term relationships. The new contacts they make at the special events they attend is another great place to meet and get connected to interesting people.

If you visualize a brick in a wall, you will see that there are six bricks that directly touch you. As you move out from those six bricks, the distance grows, and, in terms of relationship, you are now dependent on others to make or maintain the connections in that wall. The further out you get, the harder it is to stay in touch and to make deposits. Start close to home and work out from there.

What the students fail to notice is that all of these people I have mentioned are currently coming to them. And that's not something that's going to happen after they leave school. There are few times in life when this will be the case. After they get out of school, they are going to have to go out and find new people to add to their network.

At Clary Poultry & Egg, I had a good supply of healthy and headless chickens. I didn't have to roam the streets of Lubbock looking for either. That would have pushed my "acquisition costs" through the roof not to mention getting Uncle art in deep trouble with my mother. Bud's enthusiasm or ineptness was enough to make my days productive. The same is true with a student at a university or a businessperson involved in civic, religious, industry or volunteer opportunities. I encourage you, just as I do the students, to look close to you for those volunteer opportunities with nonprofits, where you can legitimately participate in not only the realization of the organization's goals but also be a part of their leadership at any level where you are comfortable. Pick up the phone and call them, and ask what you can do for them. Tell them about your skills and capabilities and passions and see if there is a match with their need. They will help you identify a committee or group within that organization and will admire your offer to participate. I have one quick caution for you as you pursue this avenue: Don't volunteer for a task that will take more time or more skill than you possess. If you accept and fail, it will be a big deduction.

Working side-by-side with people up and down the organizational chart in a nonprofit is not only a good thing to do but you will become known as a giver. You'll become known as a person who makes more deposits than withdrawals. You will be seen as a person with your hand up volunteering rather than always having your hand out asking for help. That's the reputation you want to build. Not only will you be perceived as a giving person, you will increasingly see yourself in that light. Over time, it will become more natural to give than to receive. I had the advantage of observing my mother and father and seeing how important it is to be a giver. But I also know that you can learn to be a giver if that doesn't come naturally to you at this point in your life. When people see you come into a room or walk toward them, the last thing you want them to think is, "I wonder what she wants from me today?" Or, "I wonder who he wants me to connect him with now?" That is the kiss of death in building a great network.

Find something that fits your passion, your beliefs or your purpose and then get involved. There are approximately 1.5 million registered nonprofit organizations in the United States. Surely you can find a couple that line up with your particular passions. Get your R&D department a latte and start Googling.

You also might want to attend events where the speaker is

a well-known businessperson in the community or the panel is filled with people you would like to meet. Your local universities will sponsor or co-sponsor great events throughout the year. Many of these events are attended by key executives in your community and are held right under your nose. If you have to pay $30–$40 for a ticket to sit at a table at one of the events, do it. It will be the best money you can spend.

I know it seems incongruent to mention strategy and randomness in the same sentence, but believe me when I say that they can work together for your benefit. The strategic part is identifying the nonprofit organizations and events that could be of value to you both personally and professionally. The randomness is sitting with and meeting people you don't know.

Another part of the strategy is getting a minute or two with the speaker before or after the event. That act alone is worth a lot more than the price of admission for the event. The best shot you have is at the breakfast events. People are basically lazy, and while they will always take time to attend a luncheon, they will not roll out of bed early and make it to a 7 a.m. breakfast, especially if it is a hard to access place.

I could always catch more chickens than Buddy early in the morning before he was completely alert to the task at hand. Your field of competitors that are vying for time with the speaker or other dignitaries is much smaller at that early hour, and the event organizers and sponsors appreciate the effort you've made to show up.

One of the Southern Methodist University Cox School of Business events I attended was an intimate lunch for about 1000 people featuring the CEO of a $16 billion company.

I called SMU and asked if they had any room for me at the university's table. Since I work with the School of Business as a part of the MBA Associate Board, they invited me to join them. If they had not had room, I would have purchased a ticket. This was not a random request to fill a hole in my lunch schedule. I knew who was speaking, what he was going to speak about and exactly what I wanted to ask him after the lunch. I had prepared for the meeting by attending an event the previous week and talking to someone who I knew had just given the CEO a prestigious award. Thank you Google. That enabled me to learn more about the speaker as a person outside of his business credentials and have an acquaintance in common.

After the lunch and his presentation, I stood in line to introduce myself and brought him greetings from the person who gave him the award a week earlier. Instant connection.

I asked him a quick question about one of his strategic initiatives. By the way, by carefully listening to his luncheon presentation, I knew the answer to the question and was prepared with a solution that could be communicated quickly and clearly. The response was genuine and polite, as are all of his communications. He took out a business card, wrote down the name and number of his executive assistant and asked me to give her a call. She, by the way, is the gold standard for the executive assistants that I mentioned in previous chapters.

Now, you might say that I was calculating and devious in getting that meeting. Calculating? Yes. Devious? No.

The solution was from a nonprofit organization that could bring tremendous benefit to a problem they didn't know how to solve. That is a win for everyone involved. The meeting took place within three weeks and involved people from several states including the former Governor of Wisconsin. In this instance, there was no financial upside for me in making this introduction but the potential to see lives changed for the better in every city where they did business. That was payment enough. And, once again, I made a deposit rather than a withdrawal. To get that same meeting via the normal channels of cold calling, letter writing, sending literature and everything short of setting fire to yourself in their lobby would have never worked.

I pay $45 to attend the bimonthly dinner meetings of another organization where they have local CEOs and other C-Level executives speak. Sometimes serendipity takes over and the primary reason that I attended turns out to be of secondary importance. I attended one such dinner to hear the very CEO who I just mentioned, give the very same presentation. I just wanted another opportunity to interact with him and keep my name and face top-of-mind. Besides, he is an interesting guy and the kind of servant leader we should all aspire to be. I like to support the types of organizations that hold these dinners by attending regularly, and you should be able to find something similar.

At another dinner I took a random seat next to a consultant, and the result of our conversation was a meeting that I arranged, with his help, between the CEO of a major sports equipment corporation, a representative from one of the largest wholesalers in the world and a nonprofit that could solve a problem they had collectively not been able to solve. That meeting didn't involve a single client of mine, yet it positioned me to all three organizations as both a giver and a "go to" person when something needs to happen. You have to indeed "get out there amongst 'em" if anything is going to happen. Make the investment. Take the time. Show up.

When you are in one of these networking opportunities, one of the skills you need to develop is to ask good questions and get people to talk about themselves. This whole thing about connecting and networking and being in the right places to meet the right people doesn't work unless you stop talking about your business and your travel and who you know. Think of it as a first date.

My first date with my wife was a random, blind, double date that just happened. She didn't say one word beyond "hello" the entire two hours we were thrown together. If she hadn't said "hello," I wouldn't have known she could talk at all. Her girlfriend did all the talking that night. But, I went home that night and told my mom, "Tonight I met the girl I am going to marry." Let's forget the fact that I was only 17. The wedding happened five years later. Ah ... the captivating power of silence.

Let them fall into the "I talk too much" trap, not you. Ask their advice or opinion about something, even if you have no interest in their advice. Everyone likes to pontificate and spew opinion and advice. Give them that chance. It will prime the pump and, for a fleeting moment, make them feel important. That way you can evaluate them in the light of their conversation and give you an indication of their needs and yours. Somewhere in the interaction you might just discover that this is a person who could use your help but not be able to help you at this juncture in the relationship. That's fine. Do it. Offer help. Follow through on the offer. It won't kill you, and you might just make a long-term friend who will be available for you when you are in need of something. I offered to do things around the poultry plant when I had some time to kill. Many of the things I offered to do were beyond my skill and size level. But, I offered, and that put me in a good light with everyone.

If you can find out where the person you want to meet eats on a regular basis, go there from time-to-time to see if you can have that "chance" meeting. Meet the person in the waiting area to get your car from the valet parking guys. If you're cheap, self-park but stand in the line anyway and make small talk — weather, local sports team, whatever. Nobody knows whether you valet parked or not. Do some research and find their hot button topic and have an informed opinion, fact or question.

I did this at a luncheon in Dallas and had a conversation with a multibillionaire in the energy business that led to a very productive meeting. I knew he was investing in equipment that had to be transported from the Houston ship channel to the plains of West Texas. I asked him how they were getting the equipment from the ship channel to the locations that were more than 600 miles from the port of entry. He said it was a big issue, so I asked if I could bring in someone to meet with his team who may have a better solution. I asked for his executive assistant's name and number and got the meeting. Notice, I didn't ask for his number. Big shots are more likely to give you the number of their gatekeeper than they are to give you their direct number.

Are you seeing how this works? Determine your strategy and execute. The main thing that is working against you as you attempt to start a meaningful conversation with a decision-maker is his or her lack of time. The executive you are chasing, the decision-maker on the deal you are trying to close, the head of the committee you are trying to meet, when they were lower on the food chain, they might have taken a meeting with you, but not now.

They were chickens with heads back then because they were observant and looking for ways to climb the ladder and therefore not as hard to catch. But today, we are in a business climate that makes them a bit frantic, usually overworked, sometimes panic-stricken and, to say the least, unaware of you and your need to make contact. You have got to have a strategy to identify, pursue and meet with that headless chicken.

LESSON LEARNED

Be seen as a person with your hand up rather than your hand out.

REVIEW

- Strategy is identifying the nonprofit groups and events that are beneficial to you both personally and professionally. Randomness is meeting people at those events you don't know.
- Pay close attention to your relationship capital account balances.
- Make your early deposits in those immediately around you at work, at play and at school.

SPEED IS OF THE ESSENCE

I had 75 feet to catch the chicken before it reached Texas Highway 82.

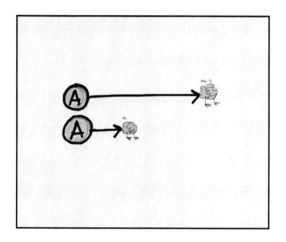

NOTHING IS MORE DEMORALIZING THAN WHEN YOU believe you have the best solution with a product or service only to hear, "I wish you would have called us a month ago. We just signed a contract with your competitor." Time and timing are two entirely different things:

- "Time" is a period during which an action, process or condition exists or continues.
- "Timing" is the spacing of events inside of a timeframe.

Both are in play as you chase the busy and overscheduled decision-makers, but "timing" is overwhelmingly the most important factor.

I had 75 feet to catch the chicken before it reached Texas Highway 82 — the high-risk zone — or the deal was all but dead or gone. How far do you have to chase down your decision-maker?

Long runways are a thing of the past in this fast-paced, hyper-over-communication age we live in. You no longer have the luxury of waiting for a deal to come together or for it to come to you. The runway to make the right connections and close business is now shorter than ever, and the traffic on that runway is deadly to your deal. You need to decide what you're going to do about that.

My clients tell me they need to get to their critical targets for meetings faster now than ever. If they don't, the risk of their not getting the order, deal or critical meeting goes up. Everyone wants to avoid risks in business or at least mitigate their risks in any way possible.

Time will eventually kill all deals!

Shortening the timeline is a huge risk mitigation factor. Many things can happen on the parking lot of a business pursuit and almost all of them are bad. The people you are chasing believe they are important, but they are clueless about why they are important to you. Getting an appointment for a busy client with a busy executive is like hitting a bullet with a bullet. Absolutely everything is in motion, and you become a part-time meeting planner, travel agent and restaurant reservationist, all within a strategic plan. And about the time you get an appointment on the books, something will change. Count on it. Be flexible. Be gracious. Be smart, and, above all, be accommodating.

At Clary Poultry & Egg, I had Buicks, Fords and Chevys in my way as I scrambled around pursuing a bird that, much like the executives you are chasing, had no idea someone was chasing him. So what's cluttering up the "parking lot" of your chase? Here are some "clutter" possibilities to consider and how to deal with each one.

How about the broader environment that is the marketplace where your targeted companies or executives work and play? That marketplace may shift underneath you and, as a result, eliminate the need for your product or service or the timeline of the original need.

Back in 1998, I bought two options to purchase two Twin

Turbo Porsches. I paid $1,000 for each option. There was a period where Porsche didn't make a Twin Turbo Model, and the demand was going to be high for the 2000. Before I had to take delivery and write a check for $228,000, I sold the options for about 10 times what I paid for them. These sales took place months before the cars shipped. Some people held on to their options thinking they would make more money later in the delivery cycle, but that didn't happen. The Porsche dealerships were prohibited from selling the new cars for more than the $114,000 list price.

When they saw what was happening in the marketplace, they discovered a loophole. They could drive the new cars a required number of miles, put them on their used car lot and sell them for whatever price the market would bear. At that point, the options were worth nothing more than a refund of your $1,000. Timing is every bit as important as being in position. The market shifted quickly for those cars, and the opportunity was gone.

Another piece of "clutter" might be that your leading-edge technology loses its edge to a competitor over time. We've discussed what your attitude and strategies in dealing with your competition should be in a previous chapter. But now consider that while you are trying to find a clear path to the CEO's office, they may trump your technology. There is never a guarantee that the timing will always be right, even when you are the first one in the door. However, the possibility of time killing your deal goes way up the longer it takes you to get to the targeted decision-maker.

A third thing that can get in your way to a successful introduction is your competitor merging with another competitor or channel partner and now makes a better case for their combined proposition. Now you are dealing with a competitor that suddenly has considerably more value than you or your client's offering.

Try to get in that door now.

How about your competition's pursuit, unlike yours, includes the use of a company for strategic introductions to provide a leveraged relationship path to the decision-maker? That means they had a better plan than their competition. From my personal client stories, when a merger is announced between two large companies, the window of time for an M&A training company to get in the door of the HR department of the acquired company is short. The sweet spot for that critical meeting is no more than two weeks following the initial announcement. At that point, your headless chicken is moving fast, and your time-to-target is short. The old saying, "He who hesitates is lost" should also say, "The company that takes too long is toast." Highway 82 and big deals wait for no man … or chicken.

Finally, it could be that the executive you're chasing may leave the company on his or her own or be fired, and you have to start pursuing a completely new target with no real avenue for connection. If you think about it, the most undervalued and under managed asset of most companies are their relationships. Very few companies have a plan that allows for building parallel relationships to mitigate the risk of the one person who holds the key relationships leaving the company. When the person leaves the relationship path to the key decision-maker, vendor, strategic partner or client, he is all but lost.

In much the same way, you need a plan for the contact you are pursuing. Put together your strategy to get to them quickly and, while you are at it, find out who is second in command, and find a way to meet and make yourself known to that person as well. The second-in-command person could, over time, be more important to you than his boss.

No headless chicken is an island.

I can't believe I said that. But, you know what I mean when I say there are always a couple of people around the key individual you are chasing who are worth knowing. Bud's backup was a guy who had absolutely no idea what he was doing, and my chicken count went up significantly when he was on duty. But, I was careful to be just as diligent when he was there as I was on a normal day. I figured that he might be the guy some day, and I better have him buttered up for that eventuality. I have already mentioned the importance of executive assistants. I am going to mention them again because they can make you or break you, and they are your conduit to the new person if the headless chicken you're chasing ends up on the highway, and, in this economic environment those chances are good.

Having said something about the "important people," let me give you a little advice on the folks who can slow you down and grind your process to a halt. Project leaders, chiefs of staff and other assorted people down the food chain can be gatekeepers to your target, and once you've contacted them, they are like a piece of gum on your shoe that just won't go away no matter how hard you try. They might be helpful to your cause, but in most cases, you will feel like you are running through wet cement waiting for it to harden beneath your feet while your deal disappears over the horizon and onto the highway. At that point you are operating at their pace, not yours. They may try to limit your access and cut off your navigation to your decision-maker.

Why?

Unlike chickens, these gatekeepers are very territorial and may see you as a threat, or they may be stalling your access until they can drain you for the information that will help solve their problem, and, at that point, there is no real need for you.

If the main decision-maker doesn't know about you or the solution you are offering, and you are dealing with someone who continues to extract more and more information from you, be careful how much you divulge on your way to that sale, engagement or deal. The fact that the boss knows you are in a process of working with the company will benefit you. If there is absolutely no way to get around them, you should use your considerable relationship skills to make your contact a hero as they take you to their boss. That is definitely a nice deposit.

Let me mention one more thing regarding this issue. If you choose to go around this gatekeeper, do so at your own peril. If you do happen to get to his or her boss or the final decision-maker and he or she sends you back down to Mr. Chewing Gum for any reason, you might as well kiss this deal goodbye. This just could be the trickiest part of the whole process and deserves your full attention.

Add about a dozen other circumstances to these few and you will have a good list of reasons why you need to be quick to the target. The longer something takes, the higher the risk of it not happening the way you wanted it to happen or it doesn't happen at all. Either way, time increases risk.

If catching a headless chicken is like hitting a bullet with a bullet, then chasing a busy executive or a complicated deal with a lot of players involved is like hitting a bullet with a bullet then hitting both with a third bullet. The more moving parts associated with the chase, the more opportunity there is for change at every level. That's why speed is of the essence.

Imagine if those cars in the parking lot of Clary Poultry & Egg were moving the whole time I was chasing the chickens. Wow! Talk about adding a new dimension to the chase. There would be a new risk of the chicken getting squashed not to mention a new risk to my long-term health. Believe me, if I thought the cars would start moving when the confused bird hit the deck, I would have doubled my efforts to catch it before it got off the dock and into the land of 6,000-pound bumper cars.

Remember, in my case, every chicken was going to die one way or another — by Bud, Buddy or the highway. In a very obtuse way, every decision-maker you chase is going to make a final decision. They are either going to choose your deal or solution or someone else's. It is going to happen.

Even though speed is a lifesaver, when it comes to catching headless chickens or nailing down critical appointments with targeted executives, there is one anomaly I would like to point out. When we talk about speed, we normally associate it more with efficiency than we do with effectiveness. But I must say that when it comes to a decision of being more "effective" (and consequently requires more work on your part) versus "efficient," choose effective every time.

- Efficient is productive without waste. Think of an efficient worker.
- Effective is producing a decided, decisive or desired effect. Think of an effective policy.

You can be more efficient and end up speeding up a worthless process or picking up speed toward the wrong target. If you are doing the wrong stuff and you work at being more efficient, you will just get to failure faster. If you are putting the wrong fertilizer on your lawn but figure out a way to spread it faster, what have you really accomplished? Your lawn dies faster.

There are hundreds of books on the shelves that will give you great advice on how to operate your life, your business, your team or your machines with greater efficiency. Bravo.

I'm all for being efficient except when it undermines being effective.

You put a recent introduction's contact information in your personal database/Rolodex by scanning in her business card or some other whiz-bang technological method. Then you quickly rip off an email saying how great it was to meet her … blah, blah, blah. And you are inwardly smiling and patting yourself on the back for being efficient in your follow-up with that person. And, indeed, you have been efficient and, yawn, ordinary in today's overly efficient business world. Congrats, you have just disappeared into the masses of efficient and un-noticed people.

And on the other end of this ho-hum email is the recipient who either gets the note or her junk filter snags it and everything goes silent. Even if she does get this highly impersonal communication, it will have very little impact and certainly will not set you apart from every other efficient person out there.

You should always be looking for advantages, both large and small and to do that you must be effective in all that you do. Effectiveness gives you a better shot at catching the headless chickens. Effective trumps efficient every time.

LESSON LEARNED

Understand the difference between "time" and "timing" in a pursuit.

REVIEW

- Choose to be effective over efficient.
- Time will kill deals.
- The direct reports of the decision-maker could be important in future pursuits.
- Clear out your parking lot clutter.

RANDOMNESS AND SERENDIPITY

I am a firm believer in serendipity — all the random pieces coming together in one wonderful moment, when suddenly you see what their purpose was all along.
—David Levithan

ALWAYS, NO MATTER HOW STRUCTURED YOUR PLAN, YOU must leave room for randomness and serendipity. And, if there was ever a random event on the planet, it was a headless bird, scrambling around a parking lot in Lubbock, Texas. Nothing could be more random than that.

Once I was driving down a Dallas street between appointments and decided to stop into the Starbucks in Highland Park Village and hang out for those 30 or so minutes. I could have just stayed in the car, made some phone calls and checked email, or caught up on the latest sports-talk drivel. It is overwhelming to think that you can actually do all of those things in a car. In this always busy coffee shop, there was a chance interaction with a person I had not seen in a while that led to a critical meeting for one of my clients. This seemingly random type meeting happens all the time. Another time I was in the throws of the same decision, stopped into a Paradise Bakery and made a connection that could prove to be invaluable to one of my new clients.

Here's the point … If you are in your car and have some time on your hands, the only person who is going to open your door and jump in that may change your life is a carjacker, and I don't think you are going to like the deal they're offering. No one you need to meet is going to come to you. I have a good friend in the commercial real estate business who frequently says, "Let's get out there amongst 'em!"

You have to get out there amongst 'em if anything is going to happen. You must always put yourself in a position to both give and receive. We have already discussed the importance of not playing out of position. This is a good example of being in position. Again, if you are in the car, about the only opportunity you are going to have to be a giver (in a face-to-face way) is to roll down your window and hand a few bucks to a panhandler. That is not exactly a great networking move. Get out of the house. Get out of the office. Get out of the car.

Now, I'm not talking about sitting in your local Starbucks with your headphones on nursing a tall latte for six hours unless you are doing research for an upcoming event or meeting. No matter where you do it, if you hide behind your computer trying to build a network that has real value through LinkedIn, email introductions, voicemails and other methods of "marketing yourself," I doubt you will achieve your goal. If you are going to a Starbucks to work, I understand that, but you must be open to making conversation with others who come and go. Go to a Starbucks or equivalent place that is in the neighborhood where your targets live, and you will have a better chance of making a connection.

Serendipity.

Randomness.

There is a certain fear of failure that some people must overcome if they are truly going to build the kind of relationships that count for something in their lives. Just as salespeople meet resistance in the selling process, you will meet some resistance in building a network. Some people will be suspicious of your generosity and will either turn down your help completely or keep their distance. That's OK. That is one of those inflection points where you turn and head in another direction. Just let the life you live, combined with your business reputation, change their minds over time. Don't waste your time trying to change them. Your time is better spent elsewhere.

For instance, spend a few dollars at the restaurant where you know the person eats who you need to meet. Meet him in the waiting area to get your car from the valet parking attendants. As we've discussed before, you can self-park but stand in the line anyway and make small talk. Scour the local newspaper, business journal or get the Eventbrite app for events where people are going to speak, buy the cheapest ticket you can get and attend. Stand in line and introduce yourself to the speaker. Do your homework beforehand about the objective of the event. Meet the organizers. Tell them how much you enjoyed the event. Ask if you can help with next year's event.

Seriously, figure out your strategy, and execute on that strategy. Always be looking for ways to stay ahead in your relationships. This is one of the places where your relationship mapping will come into play. In some of the most unlikely places, you will meet people who are in need. Be willing to help, and if you can't, at least you tried. You've just made a deposit by offering.

Whenever you invest in people by giving them something they need and then they return the favor, you need to immediately start looking for another way to invest. Think of it as rolling over the interest in a savings account.

Your goal is always to stay ahead in the giving. I am not talking about a desk calendar, ballpoint pen, scratch pad or thumb drive with your company logo on the item. I am talking about gifts of your time in the form of an introduction, a resource or whatever. This puts you in a position to ask for something if and when needed. You may never have to ask, and if you do, you may not get any help. That is the chance you have to take. But, it's more about the giving anyway not the receiving.

Always consider new ways to invest in people. People you know and people you've just met. It's like flexing a muscle to build it up. You have to train yourself to give, especially if it does not come naturally to you. Try not to leave a conversation without asking, "How can I help you?"

There may be a way you can ask that question and genuinely help the person or there may be no way you can help them. But, you have accomplished three things in just asking the question. First, you have established yourself, in their eyes, as a giver. Second, you just may have a way to help them, no matter how small or large the request. Third, you have just learned something about them that is valuable, and that is they have a need that somebody needs to meet. There is an opportunity to make a deposit. If you can't meet their need, store away the request, and if you run across someone who can help, hook 'em up.

What do I mean when I say give to people you don't know? There are people who will come across your path who have a small need. Maybe their arms are full, and they just need a little assistance with a door — someone trying to accomplish a small task where just an extra hand for a few seconds will be a great help. It will cost you a minute of your time and a little effort. But doing this on a continual basis will build the instinct to react and respond to needs. I'm not asking you to run into a burning building at this point, just be ready to give. Ready to serve. This is part of the flexing of the "giving muscles" that prepares you for meeting larger needs. And that's where you want to be.

LESSON LEARNED

The goal is to always stay ahead in relationships when it comes to deposits in the form of relationships and resources.

REVIEW

- Be out there "amongst 'em."
- Embrace randomness.
- Always remember to ask, "How can I help?"
- Look for small ways to exercise your "giving muscles" until it becomes a natural action.

KNOW WHEN TO FOLD 'EM

Of all the strategies, knowing when to quit may be the best.
— Chinese Proverb

THERE COMES A TIME WHEN YOU HAVE TO KNOW WHEN to stop chasing the chicken because the highway is a dangerous place. You have to know when to move on.

The Dip by Seth Godin offers great advice in this regard. He calls it "strategic quitting." What a great term. Sometimes either our egos or desperation drives us beyond the point of reason in a pursuit. My perseverance in chasing the chicken beyond the parking lot could have gotten me nailed by a passing car. Buddy might have been a dog, but he was smart enough to know when to quit the chase. You have to be willing to stop the chase at some point and let it die on the highway, or if it makes it across the highway, let it be someone else's pursuit.

There have been occasions where I have chased an executive to get an appointment for me or for a client long after the chase should have ended. It's like a preacher who preaches past the end of his sermon when he gets too excited. The congregation wants to beat the Baptists, who are always out on time, to the restaurants. It's 11:55, and he's making his third point for the third time and nobody's happy — except the Baptists who are already eating their desserts.

You need a self-imposed stopping place in the pursuit of every person, deal or client. There is a point of diminishing return in every pursuit with the ultimate diminishing point for me at Clary Poultry & Egg being the chrome bumper of a speeding car.

Maybe your line in the sand is a point in time. Maybe it is a financial limit beyond which you will not go to get the meeting. Another limit might be that this particular pursuit is keeping you from starting another pursuit or two or three. That's called "lost opportunity costs," and it is just as real in chasing executives as it is in the financial world.

There are signs along the road of a pursuit that are good indicators of when you should either speed up, tap the brakes or end the pursuit completely.

In the world of chasing chickens at the poultry factory those signs were that Buddy had a insurmountable lead on me, the chicken was in a place where only Buddy could reach it (under a car), the highway was too close and too busy or Uncle Art would reassign me to the tank building team (a much easier task than chasing those stupid chickens). Any of those would end my pursuit.

In the world of chasing executives the signs may be similar to the ones at the poultry factory. If your competition has what you consider to be an insurmountable lead on you, it may be time to back off the chase. That lead could take several forms. Their direct or indirect relationship with the executive could be incredibly strong to the point that you absolutely have no chance. Although this is not easy information to acquire, occasionally it can be done. If he or she is on a board with a strong friend of or related to your competitor and all other factors are equal, chances are you are not going to be the lead candidate for the business. The exception to this would be if your solutions to their problem were at least 50 percent better than the competitor that has the relationship inside track.

It could be that the pursuit has dragged on until it no longer makes sense to continue. This is an arbitrary "line in the sand" and is an individual call on each pursuit. Mostly it is a combination of gut-feel and the application of business acumen. Personally, I have a built-in curiosity that drives me to find out where the next connection will take me. That is both a good thing and a bad thing in building a network that generates business for either me or for my clients. But there is a discipline you must cultivate that allows you to both press into an opportunity long enough to see if it will pay off and, at the same time, allow you to move on when you believe it won't.

In the very rare instance the heads came off both chickens when Bud took them out of the coops, I had to make a decision of which one to chase. In a split second, I had to bring all of my chicken-chasing knowledge into play and chase the one that gave me the best chance of putting another 50 cents in my pocket. You have more than a split-second in your pursuits, but sometimes you will have to make the same choice.

About once a week, I take some time to look at the part of my personal and business network that is currently active.

- Which part of the plan is moving forward?
- Which part of it is stuck in neutral?
- Which part is headed for the ditch?
- Who in the network is a one-way street and who is a two-way street?

What I mean by that last bullet point is, who shares their contacts and is helpful and who just soaks up your help and never offers anything in response? Then I consider the amount of time and effort I think it's going to take to get each one to a successful conclusion.

- What connections are missing in the map?
- Which ones are not responding to communication?
- Is there another route to take between two circles that need to be connected?

If I can come away from that brief exercise with just one or two clear decisions, I'm happy. Back to the mapping obsession — since I am a very visual thinker, I draw circles and squares connected by lines and literally end up with a map of the current activity and then transfer that to the electronic version.

Jeff is a good friend and fellow chicken chaser. Jeff and I have an agreement that, when a BSO (Bright Shiny Object) in the form of a new deal enters our path, we will call the other one and talk it over. BSOs can distract you and cause you to shift just enough attention from important pursuits that you let both drag on way too long and neither brings success. Find someone you respect and bounce your new opportunities off him or her from time to time.

When one of my grandsons was about six or seven, I would hear him say to himself as he would be performing some task, "Focus, Will, focus." Even at that age, he knew focus was important to get something accomplished. As he's become older, the need to verbalize that mantra is no longer needed. Now it comes naturally. So ... Focus people!

LESSON LEARNED

There are signs along the road of a pursuit that will tell you when you should speed up, tap the brakes or end the pursuit completely.

REVIEW

- Be open to outside advice regarding your pursuits.
- Learn to recognize when you are on a one-way street in the relationship.
- Evaluate every pursuit in the light of all other pursuits
- Practice "strategic quitting."

CONCLUSION

IN THIS BOOK I HAVE MENTIONED ACTIONS THAT ARE AT odds with each other. Speed to the target and pace for the race, deposits and withdrawals, tilted fields and level, time and timing, efficiency and effectiveness, make plans, be flexible. Have a strategy is mentioned in the same breath as serendipity and randomness.

Every one of these actions, even though they seem to be conflicting, should be considered when you are evaluating the effectiveness of your network. As you do this week after week, you will get to the point where you can make these calculations in your head and on the fly. People, timelines, difficulties, what is a good opportunity and what is not, deposits and withdrawals, gatekeepers, events and all of the other things we've talked about will come into play. Sometimes several will come into play at the same time.

But there is hope. Consider an example that is universal ... After years of driving a car, you don't have to think individually about your speed, your position on the road, other drivers, road conditions, etc. You have done it for so long that it all flows together and is almost an unconscious effort on your part to keep moving forward and navigate to your intended destination. These things come naturally. The same is true as you grow in your experience building and navigating your network. Knowing where you should go in your network to make something happen, how to get there, what to do in preparation, how fast to move and when to stop will become instinctive. That's where you want to be.

Remember to be quick off the mark when an opportunity arises. Don't play out of position and stay in "relationship" shape. Be flexible in your pursuit of the goal, and be aware that speed is important but so is pace. Expect obstacles. Tilt the playing field in your favor by knowing your competition's strengths and weaknesses. Have a backup plan and always have two good maps. Know when to quit before you get to the highway. Look for ways to change and improve, and be open to engaging others to help you catch the headless chickens. Share some of the spoils with them if you make a deal.

Finally, as I mentioned previously, in the manufacturer's rep business, when someone would ask, "How's business?" The answer would be, "Some days chicken; some days feathers." The same was true as I pursued those headless chickens as a 9-year-old boy at Clary Poultry & Egg. And the same will be true as you pursue executives, deals, opportunities and life in general. Just make sure, as you continue the chase, you share the chicken with those who give you help and, when your chase results in feathers, just keep those to yourself.

Enjoy the chase!

ABOUT THE AUTHOR

AS FAR BACK AS I CAN REMEMBER MY PASSION HAS BEEN to help people who cross my path, find ways to improve their lives and, at the same time, benefit the greater good. My approach has been to create positive situations and connections through a platform of trust and provide connections and resources for successful outcomes.

Strategic Introductions (StrategicIntroductions.com) has been the business platform for executing my passion as well as my involvement as a director at Catapult Partners, a private equity group in Dallas, Texas. Previous to Strategic Introductions and Catapult Partners, I founded Benchmark Sales in 1982, a manufacturer's representative company in the electronic assembly and semiconductor sector that continued until the business was sold in 1998.

For more than 30 years I have been a speaker, teacher and facilitator for groups from 50 participants to 1500. Other activities have been positions on nonprofit boards, including general board membership as well as chairman of the Governor's Board. My degree is from Texas Tech in advertising art and design with minors in zoology, English literature and psychology. I served in the United States Navy — Vietnam service — and I am a current member of the Santa Barbara Chapter of The Navy League.

I have been married for 50 years to Pam Munson Humphries and together we have two daughters, Jennifer and Brooke who have gifted us with the "Fantastic Four" — our grandchildren, Kendall, Abby, Parker and Will. Life is good.

CONTACT INFORMATION

Trent Humphries

trent@strategicintroductions.com

214-676-4458

2221 Justin Road 119-342

Flower Mound, TX 75028

APPENDIX ONE

ROLODEX REVIEW AND GAP ANALYSIS

SINCE THE LIFE EXPECTANCY OF A HEADLESS CHICKEN IS somewhere between zero and 60 seconds, I had no Rolodex of chicken relationships. Hopefully the people you associate with have a somewhat longer life span, and your Rolodex doesn't turnover every 60 seconds.

My premise is that there are people currently in your personal and business Rolodex who fall into one of several categories and can compress your timeline to the kind of network you need in order to be successful. I want to take you through a quick audit of your current Rolodex followed by an exercise that will make you think in terms of "relationship communities" in which you are involved and then to a conclusion that will result in a prioritized list that you can turn into the contacts you need.

The beginning of the assessment is a work session regarding your current relationships. Set aside the time to get your current Rolodex into one place and in a form that you can get to each and every contact. You will have random business cards, names and numbers in your phone or computer and perhaps other lists you have compiled through the years. When you have these in place, take a look at the list of "communities" listed below and fill out the sheet with names of a few people in each community that you know and that know you. Here's the process.

STEP ONE

Review and document the top-of-mind contacts from these communities. Use the Advanced Thinking Document at the end of this exercise on page 129.

1. Current clients/customers (or past satisfied customers/clients)
2. Vendors to your business and personally
3. Personal relationships
4. Industry relationships
5. Country clubs/service clubs
6. School alumni
7. Partners / investors
8. Organized sports
9. Boards on which you serve
10. Religious groups
11. Charitable nonprofits
12. Attorney
13. CPA/banker.
14. Banker
15. Landlord / real estate company
16. Who is in your office building?
17. Media personalities
18. Spouse's involvements
19. Government / military officials

STEP TWO

Now that you have this list together, consider and categorize (Prioritization 1–6 with 1 being the best) each contact in the context of:

- (1) You believe they have a legitimate need for and could be a buyer of your services or product; they are accessible to you and WILL RETURN YOUR CALL!
- (2) You believe they are an influencer, not the decision-maker but a person of influence in the decision process who is inside the company or on the board you are trying to reach.
- (3) You believe they are a direct contact and person who can and will introduce you to the buyer (1) or influencer (2).
- (4) You believe they are an advocate and a person who knows and trusts you and will work on your behalf. They will give you a strong reference even though they do not directly know the person you are trying to contact for a meeting.
- (5) You believe they are simply a connector, a "Rolodex or networking" acquired contact who may be able to provide a third-party introduction that can provide access to your targeted company or decision-maker. Think LinkedIn contacts at this level.
- (6) They are a neutral contact who is a decent reference but not connected in any way to the executive or company you are pursuing for business.

STEP THREE

At this point in the assessment, look at your prioritized list with the strongest connections at the top and ask these questions:

- What would make me hesitate to call on them for business purposes? How do I overcome that hesitancy?
- What is the balance of my deposits and withdrawals in each relationship? Am I ahead or behind? What can I do to change the balance?
- Are they a good fit for my company as a client? Do I have the resources to meet their particular needs without dramatically altering my offering or the offering of my client?
- In my experience or from what I've heard, they are a one-way street or two-way street when it comes to introductions and/or connections that are helpful.

STEP FOUR

Pick **5–10** best contacts for critical meetings and … go get 'em.

APPENDIX TWO

Advanced Thinking Document for Relationship Assessment Exercise

CURRENT CLIENTS/CUSTOMERS

_____

_____

_____

_____

_____

_____

VENDORS

_____

_____

_____

_____

_____

_____

_____

INDUSTRY RELATIONSHIPS

_____

_____

_____

_____

_____

_____

_____

_____

COUNTRY CLUBS, ATHLETIC CLUBS, CIVIC CLUBS, ETC.

_____

_____

_____

_____

_____

_____

_____

SCHOOL ASSOCIATIONS/ALUMNI

_____

_____

_____

_____

_____

_____

_____

_____

PARTNERS (INVESTORS)

_____

_____

_____

_____

_____

_____

_____

ORGANIZED SPORTS (ADULT AND CHILDREN)

_____

_____

_____

_____

_____

_____

_____

_____

BOARD INVOLVEMENTS

_____

_____

_____

_____

_____

_____

_____

_____

RELIGIOUS GROUPS

_____

_____

_____

_____

_____

_____

_____

COMPETITORS/ASSOCIATED BUSINESSES

_____

_____

_____

_____

_____

_____

_____

CHARITABLE ORGANIZATIONS/NONPROFITS

_____

_____

_____

_____

_____

_____

_____

_____

ATTORNEYS

_____

_____

_____

_____

_____

_____

_____

_____

CPA/BANKERS

_____

_____

_____

_____

_____

_____

_____

LANDLORD/REAL ESTATE COMPANY

_____

_____

_____

_____

_____

_____

_____

GOVERNMENT OFFICIALS AND MILITARY PERSONNEL

_____

_____

_____

_____

_____

_____

_____

COMPANIES AND PEOPLE IN YOUR OFFICE BUILDING

_____

_____

_____

_____

_____

_____

_____

MEDIA PERSONALITIES

_____

_____

_____

_____

_____

_____

_____

SPOUSE'S INVOLVEMENTS

_____

_____

_____

_____

_____

_____

_____

CPSIA information can be obtained
at www.ICGtesting.com
Printed in the USA
LVOW12s0828070716
495000LV00001B/1/P